OIL AND ENERGY
ALTERNATIVES

Essential Viewpoints

OIL AND ENERGY
ALTERNATIVES

BY JILL SHERMAN

Content Consultant
John Freemuth, PhD
Director, Energy Policy Institute
Boise State University

ABDO
Publishing Company

CREDITS

Published by ABDO Publishing Company, 8000 West 78th Street, Edina, Minnesota 55439. Copyright © 2009 by Abdo Consulting Group, Inc. International copyrights reserved in all countries. No part of this book may be reproduced in any form without written permission from the publisher. The Essential Library™ is a trademark and logo of ABDO Publishing Company.

Printed in the United States.

Editor: Rebecca Rowell
Copy Editor: Paula Lewis
Interior Design and Production: Emily Love
Cover Design: Emily Love

Library of Congress Cataloging-in-Publication Data
Sherman, Jill.
   Oil and energy alternatives / by Jill Sherman.
      p. cm. — (Essential viewpoints)
   Includes bibliographical references and index.
   ISBN 978-1-60453-110-7
   1. Petroleum industry and trade—United States. 2. Renewable energy sources. I. Title. II. Series.
   HD9565.S444 2008
   333.8'232—dc22

                              2008007011

TABLE OF CONTENTS

Crude oil is pumped near the Rocky Mountains in Colorado.

THE RISING COST
OF OIL

O il is one of the world's most important resources. It supplies more than 60 percent of the energy in the United States. Oil, along with natural gas, powers cities, fuels cars, and heats homes. As an energy source, oil is essential to most Americans' ways of life.

In recent years, the cost of oil has increased dramatically. Because gasoline comes from oil, increases in oil prices result in higher gas prices. In 2004, the average price per gallon of gas was $1.85. That price was up to $2.27 in 2005. By spring 2008, it surpassed $4.00 per gallon. As it has become more expensive for Americans to fuel their cars and heat their homes, they have begun to take greater interest in U.S. oil and energy policies. This includes energy-efficient methods of heating and cooling buildings and fueling transportation.

The Heart of the Controversy

Oil and natural gas are finite resources—they cannot be replenished. Because the supply of oil will one day essentially run out, some people are concerned that the United States is too dependent

Oil to Gas

Petroleum, or crude oil, is a liquid found beneath the earth's surface. Crude oil is often found in conjunction with natural gas. Both oil and natural gas can be extracted and processed to use as fuel. Oil can be refined into gasoline, diesel fuel, jet fuel, and heating fuel.

on oil for its energy sources. They suggest pursuing alternative, renewable fuels as a more permanent source of energy.

Others, especially those involved in the oil industry, believe that the world's oil reserves are substantial. Oil reserves are the amount of oil known to be producible within a given period of time. In 1993, it was estimated that the world's reserves constituted a 45-year supply of oil. Because of new technologies, oil companies have been able to find and extract new

---

The 1973 Oil Crisis

Americans first realized their vulnerability to oil-producing countries during the 1970s. In 1973, in the midst of the Arab-Israeli War, oil-producing Arab countries cut oil production and halted trade with countries supporting Israel in the war, including the United States.

The loss of this oil might not have greatly affected the U.S. economy if not for the reactions of oil companies, government officials, and consumers. Members of the Organization of the Petroleum Exporting Countries (OPEC) raised their prices in response to the increased demand for oil, and oil companies were willing to pay.

Gasoline prices rose dramatically. The U.S. Energy Information Administration reports that gas averaged approximately 39¢ per gallon in 1973 and 53¢ per gallon in 1974. Adjusting for inflation, this increase is equivalent to a jump from $1.86 per gallon in 2006 to $2.36 per gallon in 2007.

In response to the crisis, the U.S. government tried to control prices and encouraged fuel conservation. In 1974, a national maximum speed limit of 55 miles per hour (88.5 km/h) was introduced by federal law to reduce consumption. Also, automobiles with increased fuel economy were manufactured. However, emphasis on oil conservation did not last long after oil prices dropped to their considerably lower prewar amounts.

supplies of oil and are optimistic about their ability to continue this trend.

Arguments about the use of oil and alternative fuels are multifaceted. Political, economic, and environmental issues weigh heavily in the debate. As the world continues to consume vast amounts of energy, these issues must be considered as scientists and researchers discover new types of energy resources and learn more efficient ways to use energy.

DETERMINING THE PRICE OF OIL

The price of oil reflects supply and demand. When oil production is reduced, supply is limited and the cost of crude oil increases. The Organization of the Petroleum Exporting Countries (OPEC) sets production rates in order to stabilize prices and ensure a steady income to its member nations.

Supply and Demand

The economic principle of supply and demand states two factors that relate directly to the price of an item. If there is a huge supply of an item but little demand for it by consumers, the price must be lowered in order to keep up sales. In contrast, if there is little supply but huge demand, sellers can increase prices because consumers are more willing to pay more for hard-to-get items.

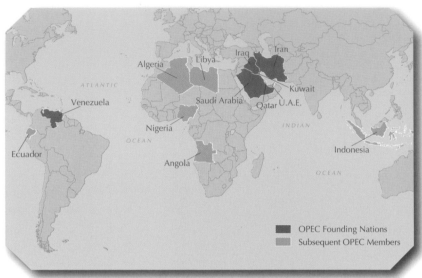

The 13 member nations of OPEC as of 2008

In 2005, OPEC member nations controlled 41.7 percent of the world's oil production. OPEC's policies have a significant effect on the price of oil, though not in every country. Non-OPEC oil-producing countries are not required to follow OPEC's production limitations.

The cost of gasoline at the pump reflects the cost of crude oil to refiners, refinery costs, marketing and distribution costs, retail costs, and taxes. In 2005, the cost of crude oil accounted for most of the U.S. price (53 percent), followed by federal and local taxes (19 percent), refining costs and profits (19 percent), and distribution and marketing (9 percent).

ACCOUNTING FOR RISING COSTS

In 2004, OPEC tightened its output, which reduced its supply and increased the price of oil. Political unrest in the Middle East, where much of the world's oil is produced, also plays a role in oil supply and costs. Nations are more apt to keep their oil during times of war or rebellion. Other oil-producing nations outside the Middle East face similar issues.

Problems abroad dramatically affect U.S. oil prices because the country imports approximately 58 percent of its oil. Oil produced in the United States is not subject to the production restrictions of OPEC, but U.S. reserves cannot meet the country's demand for oil.

OPEC

OPEC was founded in 1960 by Iran, Iraq, Kuwait, Saudi Arabia, and Venezuela. OPEC was founded in order for oil-producing countries to establish production rates and prices.

As of 2008, OPEC had 13 member nations. The five founding nations have been joined by Qatar, Indonesia, Socialist People's Libyan Arab Jamahiriya (Libya), United Arab Emirates, Algeria, Nigeria, and Angola. Ecuador rejoined OPEC in November 2007. Gabon was once part of OPEC but is no longer a member.

As its reserves are depleted, the United States must rely more heavily on imported oil.

Weather can also affect oil supplies and fuel prices. In September 2005, the U.S. Gulf Coast was hit by two hurricanes: Katrina and Rita. Approximately 28 percent of domestic oil is produced in this region. The oil industry faced a serious setback. High winds and waves damaged offshore rigs, refineries, and pipelines in the area. These rigs were temporarily shut down for repairs. The impact of these hurricanes cut the supply of domestic oil to the United States. The U.S. Energy Information Administration estimated that the U.S. oil supply was reduced by 1.4 million barrels a day. This reduction caused gas prices to jump in the days following the hurricanes.

Americans are eager to see oil costs reduced. However, analysts such as Phil Flynn of Alaron Trading Corporation do not foresee the price of oil decreasing

U.S. Reserves

According to U.S. Energy Information Administration estimates, domestic reserves of crude oil have been steadily decreasing since 1970 when they peaked at 39 billion barrels. As of 2006, estimates put U.S. reserves at 21 billion barrels. The United States uses approximately 20 million barrels a day. If new sources of oil are not found, supply will struggle to meet demand. As a result, the cost of oil will continue to rise.

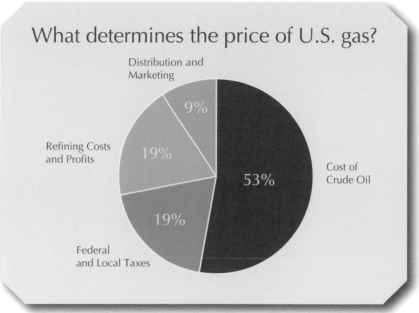

What determines the price of U.S. gas?

Distribution and Marketing

9%

Refining Costs and Profits

19%

Cost of Crude Oil

53%

Federal and Local Taxes

19%

The price of gas in the United States is determined by several factors. In 2005, the cost of crude oil accounted for more than half the price.

dramatically in the near future. According to Flynn, "We're in a new era of high gas prices. . . . The shock value of $2 gasoline has gone away. It's a part of life. How long that can go on we don't know."[1]

REDUCING U.S. DEPENDENCY ON FOREIGN OIL

Opinions differ as to what has caused the cost of foreign oil to rise. However, many people agree that the way to combat this increase is for the United States to reduce its dependency on foreign oil.

For some, this means increasing the number of refineries within the United States and excavating new land for reserves. These measures will be necessary if the United States is to keep up with its growing demand for oil, which the U.S. Department of Energy predicted in 2004 would increase 43 percent by 2025.

Not everyone supports increasing U.S. oil production. For some, the solution to U.S. oil problems is using alternative and renewable energy sources such as the sun, wind, and biodiesel fuel. A move to alternative fuel could offer a more permanent source of energy and head off a potential oil crisis. According to Georgetown University Government Professor Robert J. Lieber, "When the market is running tight, anything—whether it's a hurricane, or war, or revolution, or terrorism—can precipitate a crisis."[2]

An oil platform was damaged by Hurricane Katrina in the Gulf of Mexico near Dauphin Island, Alabama, in late August 2005.

Car ownership has increased dramatically in China, resulting in clogged roads. Laws have been created to reduce chronic traffic jams in Beijing.

Signs Pointing to an Oil Crisis

Knowledge that the world's oil supply cannot be replenished has raised concerns. No matter how much oil is below the earth's surface, the supply is not infinite. The rising cost of oil could be viewed as a sign that reserves are being depleted. The outlook from this standpoint is bleak. As more nations become industrialized, oil demand increases. With reserves being depleted, the oil industry may not be able to meet the needs of industrialized nations.

Increased demand could make it more profitable to extract oil from hard-to-reach reservoirs for a time. Oil is a desirable resource because it is relatively inexpensive. However, if reserves from which oil can be extracted economically are not found, prices will continue to increase as supply decreases. At a certain point, consumers will demand oil alternatives more than oil when the cost becomes unbearable. The world may soon experience a full-blown energy crisis.

Oil Use Increasing Worldwide

The U.S. Energy Information Administration expects that world demand for oil will grow by 50 percent by 2025. Industrialization increases the demand for oil. As

Effects of Oil Depletion

"The Peaking of World Oil Production: Impacts, Mitigation, and Risk Management" study was prepared for the U.S. Department of Energy. It presents some of the effects of oil depletion. According to the study, if world oil peaks, industrialized nations could experience increased costs for the production of goods and services, inflation, unemployment, reduced demand for products other than oil, and a lower capital investment.

more countries have become industrialized, oil has become a more valuable resource. Global demand has increased competition for oil, most notably in China and India. China, which has more than 1 billion citizens, has experienced a sudden burst in car ownership and become the third-largest consumer of cars. In 2006, car ownership by individuals grew 33.5 percent. In 2007, total vehicle sales boomed almost 22 percent to a record 8.79 million. China's National Development and Reform Commission predicts that the Chinese will have 55 million vehicles by 2010.

"One of the key strategic issues facing the United States is how to insure continued access to OPEC oil when other countries are also importing more fuel," says John Cassidy, an economic and finance reporter for *The New Yorker*.[1] Cassidy also notes that global demand for oil has increased by one-fifth over the past ten years.

Without more oil production, this added demand could increase prices dramatically. A drastic hike could push the price to the

Cars in China

In the mid-1980s, bicycles dominated China's roads with approximately 500 million cyclists. The number of cyclists has dropped dramatically as car ownership has become more affordable. In 2004, approximately 27 million automobiles were on China's roads, and that number is expected to continue to increase.

Workers at an oil-extracting field in Yan'an, in northwest China

"tipping point," the price at which consumers will reduce their consumption or change their spending habits. When the price of gas first topped $3.00 per gallon, there was a notable difference in the types of cars that were purchased. Demand for the once-popular sport utility vehicles (SUVs) plunged because they have poor gas mileage. In September 2007, General Motors (GM) and Ford posted declines in SUV sales of 24 percent and 20 percent, respectively. In addition, light-truck sales dropped 30 percent for GM and 28 percent for Ford.

Consumers have also changed their driving habits in response to increased gas prices. In 2007, the *Daily Fuel Economy Tip* asked, "Have sustained gas prices above $2.50 per gallon changed the amount of driving you do?"[2] Approximately 25 percent of respondents said gas prices had not changed their driving habits, but more than double this amount—69 percent—responded affirmatively.

Even with such changes by consumers, the demand for oil continues to grow. If oil production is increased to meet the demand for fuel, reserves could quickly be depleted. Many estimates say that at the current rate of consumption, the world may run out of oil in 40 years. If global demand continues to rise, oil supplies could be depleted much sooner.

RESERVES OVERESTIMATED

Many methods are used to estimate the amount of oil left in reserves. However, analysts must guess or make assumptions for numerous unknown factors. As a result, different estimates of reserves are often calculated from the same information.

Making precise calculations is made more difficult by nations that report inaccurate reserves for political reasons or to maintain business relationships. L. F. Ivanhoe is a geologist and president of Novum Corporation, an international energy exploration consulting firm. According to Ivanhoe, many nations have been known to report the same numbers from year to year and others appear to be approximations. Ivanhoe states:

> *There is no way to check on the accuracy of foreign reports. To many foreign ministries . . . requests for reserve data is either a sensitive state secret or a nuisance chore no one is critically concerned about.* [3]

Speculation is also an issue. As Ivanhoe notes:

> *Well-intentioned but irresponsible scientists who continue to discuss resources [the theoretical presence of oil] instead of reserves [accessible, producible sources] may be a significant cause of our government's lack of realistic energy policies.* [4]

Regardless of the reason for underestimation, if reserves are less than analysts have estimated, a crisis could happen sooner than expected.

Oil Shortage in Saudi Arabia

Matthew Simmons is an energy investment banker and author of *Twilight in the Desert*. He believes that Saudi Arabia's oil production is on the verge of peaking. Although Saudi Arabia has said it will continue to keep the market supplied with oil, Simmons believes the country is "relying on the fact that for seventy years they've been able to keep this miracle going with a small number of fields . . . there's a real risk that their current rate of production can't be sustained for much longer." [5]

INSIGNIFICANT NEW RESERVES

Largest Oil Fields

The four largest oil fields in 2005 from largest to smallest were:
- Ghawar in Saudi Arabia
- Cantarell in Mexico
- Burgan in Kuwait
- Daqing in China

Many analysts agree that numerous oil reservoirs have yet to be discovered. But analysts who consider the world to be on the verge of an oil crisis do not believe that these reserves will greatly affect the world's oil supply. They say that the world's largest oil fields have been discovered because larger fields are easier to find. Additional oil discoveries would certainly help, but they may not meet the growing global demand. Meanwhile, the world's oil supply continues to diminish.

Some analysts say that such a decline would encourage oil exploration and discovery. However, according to John Attarian of the University of Michigan:

> Whether or not more oil will be found depends, ultimately, on whether or not it exists, which is a matter of geology, not economics. Arguing that if price gets high enough there will be massive oil discovery is like telling drought-stricken farmers that when the price of water gets high enough, it will rain.[6]

OIL PRODUCTION NEARING ITS PEAK

Some analysts predict that world oil production is about to reach its peak. That is, oil production will no longer increase from year to year but will begin to decline. According to Attarian, "After peak, instead of supply adjusting upward to meet demand, as it has so far, demand will have to adjust *downward* to meet supply."[7]

Six countries peaked in 2001 alone. Analysts are able to compare current oil production to historical data of other countries that have peaked in the past. This data goes back to

Hubbert's Peak

At a meeting of the American Petroleum Institute in 1956, M. King Hubbert presented his theory on peak oil. Hubbert was a geoscientist who worked at the Shell research laboratory in Texas. His theory, "Hubbert's Peak," states that oil, as a nonrenewable resource, will eventually peak in its production and begin to decline.

Hubbert predicted that oil production in the United States would peak between 1965 and 1970. U.S. oil production reached its peak in 1971. Hubbert also predicted that worldwide oil production would reach its peak in 2000. Most experts agree that worldwide oil production has not peaked. Those who support Hubbert's theory expect that it will peak in the near future. Princeton University Geology Professor Kenneth Deffeyes states, "World production is flat now."[8] Most new estimates put the peak at no later than 2010, although there are analysts who predict the date to be 2035.

Hubbert's theory assumes that most of the world's oil supply has been discovered. Critics believe new technologies will allow more oil to be found and extracted than anticipated. For this reason, many analysts believe the world's peak oil production is a long way off.

Break-even Price

The cost to extract a single barrel of oil is the break-even price. When deciding whether to begin drilling, oil companies establish the break-even price first.

the 1950s when Austria peaked. Analysts must look at current production and found reserves not yet in production to estimate the reserves to be discovered. Because reserves that have not been discovered are unknown, estimates for when oil will peak are highly controversial. While estimates vary, many analysts expect world oil production will peak soon—perhaps as early as 2010. During this decline in production, it will eventually cost more to extract oil than the revenue selling it can bring. It simply will not make financial sense for an oil company to extract oil when doing so will cost more than what the company can earn by selling it. When this occurs, oil production will decline even though there may be billions of barrels worth of oil remaining beneath the earth's surface.

*Oil is pumped through pipelines in the Czech Republic.
More than half of the country's imported oil comes
from Russia. The rest comes from Germany.*

The drilling ship Deep Sea Discovery *is Chevron's newest project, located 140 miles (225 km) off the coast of Louisiana.*

Signs Pointing to No Oil Crisis

*D*espite what some analysts have determined, many experts believe that the world's oil supply is abundant. They point to research that indicates reserves are increasing even with the growing demand for oil. Although oil is always being extracted and used, new sites for oil extraction are continually being discovered.

In addition, engineers in the oil industry are confident that new technologies will help increase oil production and find new reservoirs. If the oil supply does begin to dwindle, it will spark interest in further developing these technologies. According to Peter W. Huber and Mark P. Mills, authors of *The Bottomless Well*, "Fuels recede, demand grows, efficiency makes things worse . . . it will all run out but we will always find more."[1]

PAST PREDICTIONS WRONG

For decades, experts have predicted that an oil shortage is approaching. The U.S. Geological Survey predicted in 1919 that world oil production would reach its peak by 1928. In 1956, it was predicted that oil would peak in 2000. In 1977, President Jimmy Carter warned Americans that "we could use up all the proven reserves of oil

Reliance on Oil

Some economists believe that the world will not face an oil crisis, in part, because we are not reliant solely on oil as a source of energy. Oil consumption will be offset by increased use of other energy sources, and oil reserves will last much longer than some predictions. Walter E. Williams is a former chairman of the Department of Economics at George Mason University. According to Williams, "Oil as a source of energy has been in decline. In 1980, oil was 45 percent of energy consumption; today, it's 34 percent, yielding ground to natural gas, coal and nuclear energy."[2]

in the entire world by the end of the next decade."[3] Predictions of oil shortages have repeatedly failed to come true.

Many of those in the oil industry are not worried by predictions of shortages. Historically, new oil fields are discovered and new technologies make accessing known reserves easier and more affordable. They have seen oil production increase when experts have forecasted declines. Oil industry executives have no reason to believe this pattern will not be repeated.

New Reserves

As oil is extracted and refined from one location, new oil fields in other locations are ready

Past Predictions

Wood was the most widely used energy source during the seventeenth century. As Europe became more industrialized, wood was in high demand. The supply dwindled, and the cost of wood rose as forests were exhausted. Europe feared that it would face an energy crisis. People began to look for new energy sources. Coal soon replaced wood as the dominant energy source. However, in 1865, economist William Stanley Jevons began to predict the supply of coal would soon be depleted. By the early twentieth century, use of crude oil was on the rise.

to take over. Russia is aggressively pursuing new oil fields. In 2007, according to the U.S. Energy Information Administration, Russia produced 9.7 million barrels of oil a day, which was an increase in production. It is the highest oil-producing country after Saudi Arabia. Russia is also pursuing oil exploration in the Arctic, a region believed to have enormous oil reservoirs. And in South America, Brazil has found offshore oil.

On September 6, 2007, the *New York Times* reported that a significant oil discovery was made in the Gulf of Mexico: between 3 billion and 15 billion barrels of oil. At the time of the discovery, U.S. reserves were approximately 29 billion barrels. This discovery could potentially increase U.S. reserves by half.

Underdeveloped Reserves

According to Leonardo Maugeri of Italian energy company ENI, oil resources in Iran, Iraq, Kuwait, Oman, Qatar, Saudi Arabia, and the United Arab Emirates are relatively underdeveloped. This is due, in part, to Western oil companies having been thrown out of the countries in the 1970s. Though these countries gained independence, they lost access to new technological developments. For example, Maugeri states:

> [In Iraq] three-dimensional seismic surveys, deep and horizontal drilling, and advanced techniques for recovering crude have never been used, even though these practices have revolutionized the oil industry in the rest of the world since the 1980s.[4]

In addition, Saudi Arabia, the world's largest oil-producing country, has great potential to increase its production. According to Maugeri, Saudi Arabia has not been fully explored. It is possible that Saudi Arabia could house much more oil than its known reserves. Introducing new technological advances to countries such as Saudi Arabia and Iraq could dramatically increase oil reserves.

OPEC oil and energy ministers pose at an OPEC conference
in Abu Dhabi, United Arab Emirates, on December 5, 2007.

New Technology

New technologies have the potential to increase oil production, make extraction more affordable, and help find new reserves. Many economists believe that governments and oil executives will attend to developing new technologies to make these things possible if the price of oil approaches its tipping point.

According to Leonardo Maugeri, a senior vice president for the Italian energy company ENI:

Despite all the predictions of impending catastrophic shortages, the world still possesses immense oil reserves. "Proven" reserves alone, more than 1.1 trillion barrels, could fuel the world economy for 38 years even at current rates of consumption. And this figure understates potential production, because the accepted definition of proven reserves includes only those reserves that can be exploited with currently available technology at conservatively projected prices. An additional 2 trillion barrels of "recoverable" reserves are not classified as proven but will probably meet that standard in a few years as technological improvements, increased knowledge of the subsoil, and the economic incentive created by higher oil prices (or lower extraction costs) come into play.[5]

The world's known oil reserves are immense. What is needed is the means to extract and refine these

Applied Technology

In March 2007, Jad Mouawad reported for the *New York Times* on innovations in the oil industry. He wrote, "Within the last decade, technology advances have made it possible to unlock more oil from old fields, and, at the same time, higher oil prices have made it economical for companies to go after reserves that are harder to reach."[6]

Thanks to new technology, the Kern River oil field in California has increased production from 10,000 barrels to 85,000 barrels a day. The Duri oil field in Indonesia has increased production from 65,000 barrels to 200,000 barrels a day. New technologies will soon be applied to the Means oil field in Texas—production is expected to double.

Top Oil-producing Countries

The top ten oil-producing countries' production in millions of barrels per day in 2006, according to the U.S. Energy Information Administration:
1. Saudi Arabia: 10.7
2. Russia: 9.7
3. United States: 8.4
4. Iran: 4.1
5. China: 3.8
6. Mexico: 3.7
7. Canada: 3.2
8. United Arab Emirates: 2.9
9. Venezuela: 2.8
10. Norway: 2.8

reserves—and to do so in the most economical way possible.

OPEC POLICIES FRIGHTEN CONSUMERS

OPEC countries periodically meet to fix their prices or output—each of which determines the other. By limiting output, OPEC can increase its prices and revenues. However, although less oil is produced, there is no global oil shortage. OPEC could decide to increase its output at any time. The United States has no say in the matter. This lack of control leaves many Americans struggling when the price of oil spikes.

The United States and other Western nations have a good deal of interest in OPEC nations. The United States protects OPEC nations in order to ensure access to their oil. However, despite this protection, OPEC continues to restrict its output. It has no obligation to the United States. The result of restricted output is higher prices for consumers, including fuel to power vehicles and to heat homes.

A man pumps gas at a station in San Jose, California, in January 2008. The recent increase in the cost of oil is reflected in the price.

Gas is a vital resource for many Americans. Increased prices have not stopped consumers from filling their tanks.

POLITICS OF OIL: U.S. DOMESTIC POLICIES

*M*any Americans are concerned about reducing the price of oil. When there is a sudden increase in the price of oil, the issue receives more attention. This is particularly so during times of greater oil use: in the summer, when travel is more common, and in the winter, when homes need heat. Americans often look to the federal government to find ways to lower prices.

U.S. legislation plays an important role in the cost of oil, as do environmental regulations. The U.S. government often establishes new energy policies to satisfy the needs of the nation and its citizens. The policies that are instituted—and whether they will significantly affect the current structure—is a matter of debate.

Environmental Regulations

In the United States, the oil industry is required to meet a variety of environmental regulations. These regulations aim to please those who fear the environmental damage of an oil spill. Many Americans support actions to limit the prevalence of oil refineries in their communities. But environmental regulations often limit the oil industry's ability to produce oil domestically.

Millions of acres of U.S. land are restricted from oil activity even though oil is known to exist there.

Top U.S. Oil Fields

In January 2008, the top five oil fields in the United States were:
1. Prudhoe Bay, Alaska
2. East Texas, Texas
3. Wilmington, California
4. Midway-Sunset, California
5. Kuparuk River, Alaska

Requests by oil companies to build new refineries and pipelines are often met with opposition by environmental lobbyists. For this reason, no new refineries have been built on U.S. land since 1976. All of this makes the United States more reliant on imported oil. U.S. policies currently do not favor domestic oil production.

ENERGY POLICY ACT

On August 8, 2005, President George W. Bush signed the Energy Policy Act of 2005. The first national energy plan instituted in more than ten years, the act seeks to promote "dependable, affordable, and environmentally sound production and distribution of energy for America's future."[1]

According to the White House, the act aims to improve energy efficiency by providing consumers with tax cuts for making energy-efficiency changes to their homes and by setting efficiency standards on new appliances, such as water heaters and furnaces. Tax credits are also available for consumers who purchase energy-saving vehicles such as hybrid, clean-diesel, and fuel-cell automobiles. In addition, the act promotes diversifying the U.S. energy supply with solar, wind, and biomass energy. It also

President George W. Bush applauds the U.S. Congress for passing the Energy Policy Act of 2005.

encourages greater use of renewable fuels, such as ethanol and biodiesel.

The act has gained support for its efforts to increase energy efficiency and explore new technologies. Caspar W. Weinberger, former U.S. secretary of defense and a reporter for *Forbes*, writes of the act:

> [It] will encourage additional, cleaner and more reliable sources of energy, something we have urgently needed for far too many years. This bill is truly comprehensive. . . . it encourages a broad range of new explorations in a major effort to try to move us away from our heavy dependence on imported fossil fuels. [2]

CRITICISM OF THE ENERGY POLICY ACT

Critics of the Energy Policy Act of 2005 note that it does little to reduce U.S. dependency on foreign oil or the cost of oil. Reducing the cost of oil is one of the measure's long-term goals. However, it is an issue most Americans would like resolved sooner. Critics doubt that the act will affect the price of oil.

Because the United States imports approximately 58 percent of its oil, analysts believe the energy bill can do little more than slow the rate of dependency on foreign oil.

Jimmy Carter on Energy

In 1977, President Jimmy Carter spoke to Americans about the importance of taking energy policies seriously:

I know that some of you may doubt that we face real energy shortages. The 1973 gasoline lines are gone, and our homes are warm again. But our energy problem is worse tonight than it was in 1973 or a few weeks ago in the dead of winter. It is worse because more waste has occurred, and more time has passed by without our planning for the future. And it will get worse every day until we act.

The oil and natural gas we rely on for 75 percent of our energy are running out. In spite of increased effort, domestic production has been dropping steadily at about six percent a year. Imports have doubled in the last five years. Our nation's independence of economic and political action is becoming increasingly constrained. Unless profound changes are made to lower oil consumption, we now believe that early in the 1980s the world will be demanding more oil than it can produce.[3]

According to Ben Lieberman of the Heritage Foundation, an educational and research institute, "We'll be dependent on the global market for more than half our oil for as long as we're using oil, and the energy bill isn't going to change that."[4]

In addition, critics feel the act focuses too much on using domestic oil, which is in limited supply. Kevin Knobloch of the Union of Concerned Scientists believes the best way for the United States to reduce dependency on foreign oil is for the federal government to require improved fuel economy standards on new vehicles, a measure the energy act ignores.

CORPORATE AVERAGE FUEL ECONOMY

The U.S. Congress first enacted Corporate Average Fuel Economy standards on new model cars and light trucks in 1975. This includes SUVs, vans, and trucks, though some SUVs and trucks over a certain weight are exempt from complying.

The Bush Administration has imposed new fuel economy standards. By 2011, even large SUVs will be required to meet the

"Our dependence on foreign oil is like a foreign tax on the American dream, and that tax is growing every year."[5]

—*President George W. Bush, 2005*

new standards in order to be sold in the United States. The National Highway Traffic Safety Administration estimates that the new standards will save more than 250 million gallons (946 million L) of gas a year.

Automotive makers complain that the new standards are unmanageable and that they will be forced to discontinue some of their larger model SUVs. Ron Gettelfinger, president of United Automobile, Aerospace, and Agricultural Implement Workers of America (UAW), states:

> *Forcing automakers into a product mix that does not fit the United States market will not improve fuel economy or protect the environment—and the large costs involved will be an economic disaster for automakers, workers and retirees.*[6]

Despite these complaints, in November 2007, courts in California ordered that fuel economy standards be raised for light trucks. Currently, standards for light trucks are far below those for cars. Benefits of such an increase in standards include decreased emissions and decreased demand for oil.

As UAW president, Ron Gettelfinger represents workers in the auto
industry by promoting actions that support the environment,
automakers, and workers.

*A U.S. Army soldier walks toward a burning oil well
in southern Iraq in March 2003.*

POLITICS OF OIL:
INTERNATIONAL RELATIONS

espite intentions to make oil a domestic
issue, the United States continues to rely
on imported oil. As of 2007, the country imports
more than half of its oil. Because of this dependency,
it is important to maintain favorable political

relationships with the supplying countries.

The United States is heavily invested in the ever-changing political alliances of the Middle East, the location of the majority of OPEC nations. The U.S. government frequently takes on the role of peacekeeper there. Because exporting oil is more difficult during times of war, the United States wants to ensure continued access to that oil.

Maintaining favorable relationships with oil-supplying countries is a goal of other nations as well. The United States faces increasing competition for oil from countries such as China and India. Also, China and Russia are aggressively expanding their oil interests with a series of deals that some political analysts see as a play for global power. These deals also increase competition for oil,

Top U.S. Oil Suppliers

According to the U.S. Energy Information Administration, the top ten crude oil suppliers to the United States in millions of barrels per day as of March 2008 were:
1. Canada: 1.7
2. Saudi Arabia: 1.5
3. Mexico: 1.2
4. Nigeria: 1.1
5. Venezuela: .9
6. Iraq: .8
7. Angola: .4
8. Algeria: .2
9. Ecuador: .2
10. Brazil: .2

which threatens the United States economically—
competition increases prices and makes oil less
available to the nation.

The War in Iraq

On March 19, 2003, President George W.
Bush announced that a U.S.-led coalition would
invade Iraq. He cited failed weapons inspections
and Iraq's potential holding of weapons of mass
destruction as reasons for the invasion. The U.S.
government maintains that the war in Iraq began to
remove Saddam Hussein, a dangerous dictator, from
power and to spread democracy in the Middle East.
However, the view that the Iraq war was motivated by
oil is a popular one in the Middle East.

Regardless of its role in motivating the war in
Iraq, oil will play a large role in rebuilding Iraq.
With proven reserves second only to Saudi Arabia,
the country has a huge potential to produce oil.
But economic sanctions have prevented Iraq from
modernizing its equipment and infrastructure. The
U.S. Energy Information Administration reports
that Iraq's estimated 2003 prewar oil capacity was
3 million barrels of oil per day. It is estimated that
Iraq could easily double its output by implementing

modern technology. Dramatic changes within its government would need to precede the production increase.

Before Iraq's oil industry can be improved, all military violence must end. U.S. military presence in Iraq upsets many groups, and violence continues to erupt. Several politicians consider it unwise for U.S. military personnel to pull out of Iraq until there is political and economic stability. This stability will be necessary to encourage investment in Iraq's oil industry,

Iraq

During the Iran-Iraq War (1980–1988), the United States supported Iraq. This support established Saddam Hussein as Iraq's leader. Iraq won the war, but oil wells were severely damaged, which dramatically lowered production. Iraq also had about $80 billion in war debts.

Following the war, Hussein focused on the neighboring country of Kuwait. Iraqis believe Kuwait was meant to be included in Iraq's borders after World War I. In addition, Kuwait's oil resources were far greater than Iraq's. Claiming Kuwait would put Iraq in a better position to intimidate other neighboring nations into relieving Iraqi war debts.

Iraq invaded Kuwait on August 2, 1990. The United States and many other nations set up an economic embargo against Iraq. They demanded that Hussein pull his troops out of Kuwait immediately. He refused. On January 17, 1991, President George H. W. Bush launched air strikes against Iraq with Operation Desert Storm. Iraq agreed to a cease-fire in February 1991. Economic sanctions imposed after the war limited Iraq's army and its ability to export oil. An oil-for-food program was established by the United Nations in 1995, but the Iraqi population continued to suffer from food shortages.

says Daniel Yergin, chairman of Cambridge Energy Research Associates. According to Yergin, "No company will write a check for a million dollars without some sense of stability."[1] Iraqi oil fields and refineries remain military targets. Investors are unlikely to come forward without U.S. forces to maintain order.

Saudi Oil

Saudi Arabia is the world's leading oil-producing country, supplying 10.7 million barrels of oil per day. It also holds about one-fourth of the world's known reserves. Saudi Arabia's oil industry is technologically advanced and has the capacity for extra production in times of war and crisis.

The United States relies on Saudi Arabia for approximately 1.5 million barrels of oil per day. The two countries have a long-standing political relationship. Saudi Arabia supplies the United States with oil in times of crisis, and the United States comes to Saudi Arabia's aid during threats of war. When Iraq invaded Kuwait in 1990, the United States sent troops to Saudi Arabia to defend the country from Iraqi forces. By August 31, more than 60,000 U.S. troops were deployed to Saudi Arabia

Saudi Arabian Oil Minister Ali al-Naimi

as part of Operation Desert Shield. In turn, Saudi Arabia supplied the United States with the oil it would not receive from the warring Iraq and Kuwait.

Saudi oil fields remain highly protected. Saudi Arabia spent an estimated $1.2 billion between 2002 and 2004 to increase security. It maintains 25,000 to 30,000 troops to protect its oil infrastructure.

Saudi Oil during World War II

The United States began its relationship with Saudi Arabia during World War II. At the time, the U.S. government was worried about sustaining its oil production and supporting its allies during the war. Oil was more important during World War II than it had been in previous wars. It was needed to power tanks, ships, airplanes, and other weapons. It was an important resource in winning the war. The United States became more reliant on oil from the Middle East during this period. Also, it was a way to increase national security by relieving pressure on domestic oil production.

According to Saudi oil executive Abdullatif Othman, "For years, Saudi Arabia has recognized the importance of protecting its vital facilities, long before the recent terrorist actions."[2] The large amounts of oil in reserves and Saudi Arabia's ability to produce this oil make it an important source for the United States—now and in the future.

Saudi Arabia is more than willing to provide the United States with oil. However, evidence suggests that the Saudi government uses some of its oil profits to fund terrorism. Osama bin Laden, the leader of the terrorist attacks of September 11, 2001, and 15 of the 19 members of the attack were Saudi nationals. The view that Saudi Arabia uses its oil revenues and position in OPEC to promote anti-American policies and fund terrorism is becoming increasingly accepted among political analysts.

Members of the media point to the $30 billion the United States spends on Saudi oil annually as evidence that the United States is "financing both sides of the war on terrorism."[3] Numerous political analysts believe that the United States would do best to limit its reliance on Saudi oil.

THE CHINA PROBLEM

As of 2006, China had an estimated 16 billion barrels of oil in reserves. It was once expected that China would be able to sustain itself on this supply, but the country has seen dramatic economic growth in the past decade. However, its oil-producing capacity is not expected to grow much in the coming decade. China is the world's largest oil-consuming country after the United States. If China continues to grow economically, it will need to look for external oil sources.

China is strategically establishing a presence in the Middle East. Through investments, the China Petroleum and Chemical Company is helping nations such as Iran and Saudi Arabia develop their natural gas resources. China is especially interested

Oil-consuming Countries

According to the U.S. Energy Information Administration, the top ten oil-consuming countries in millions of barrels per day in 2006 were:
1. United States: 20.6
2. China: 7.3
3. Japan: 5.2
4. Russia: 2.9
5. Germany: 2.7
6. India: 2.5
7. Brazil: 2.3
8. Canada: 2.2
9. South Korea: 2.2
10. Saudi Arabia: 2.1

in developing relationships with Middle Eastern countries such as Iran and Iraq, which the United States has economic sanctions against. China is also establishing economic relationships with oil-producing countries such as Canada, Russia, Sudan, and Venezuela. According to Irwin M. Stelzer of the Hudson Institute's Center for Economic Policy Studies, "China clearly aims to position itself as an alternative to America as an ally and armorer [protector] of countries that oppose U.S. foreign policy."[4]

Many political experts see China's expansion as a threat to the United States. According to author Robert Dreyfuss, "Even a novice . . . knows that who controls oil controls the world. And in this case, America's rival for control of oil is, first and foremost, China."[5]

China's Yaha oil field is the country's largest condensate oil production base.

Oil spills are hazardous to sea life. These sea lions were covered in oil following the Exxon Valdez *accident in March 1989.*

OIL AND THE ENVIRONMENT

O il is a natural resource buried deep within the earth. Extraction, transportation, and use of oil as a source of energy threaten the environment. Burning oil results in carbon emissions. The effect of these emissions on the environment concerns the United States and other countries. Some question how great the environmental effects of carbon emissions will become and whether significant changes in global energy policies are justified. Others predict serious repercussions, such as global warming, triggered by climate changes from carbon and other factors.

OIL SPILLS

Oil spills can occur during any stage of production. Most often, oil spills are due to human error. They can also occur because of hurricanes and other natural disasters, or because of terrorist attacks. Oil spills can have a devastating effect on the environment. Typically, oil floats on water and spreads rapidly, which creates an oil slick. Fragile ecosystems are harmed by oil slicks, and fish, birds, and other wildlife are often killed because of them.

The largest U.S. oil spill was in 1989 off the Alaskan shore. Approximately 11 million gallons of crude oil was spilled when the *Exxon*

Acid Rain

Sulfur and nitrogen oxides that result from burning fossil fuels can react with air and water vapor to form acid rain. The acidic content of rain can raise the pH levels (acid levels) of rivers and lakes, killing microorganisms and fish. Plant life can also be damaged by high pH levels in the rain, and the nutrient value of the soil can be depleted.

Man-made structures also have been visibly damaged by acid rain. The Parthenon in Athens, Greece, and the Taj Mahal in Agra, India, both show signs of deterioration.

Valdez oil tanker ran aground on a reef in Prince William Sound on March 24. This oil spill killed thousands of animals—birds, otters, and seals.

The methods used to contain a spill and remove the oil vary and depend on the location of the spill. Chemicals, microbes, and vacuums are often used to remove the oil. Spills can be very costly to clean up. Exxon Corporation paid several billion dollars to clean up the spill in Prince William Sound. Environmental scientists say the effects of that spill can still be seen, and they do not expect the region to recover until 2019.

Carbon Emissions

Burning fossil fuels causes the most serious environmental effects. When fossil fuels such as oil and coal are burned, carbon is released into the atmosphere. The carbon combines with oxygen to form a gas called carbon dioxide. Levels of carbon dioxide in the atmosphere have grown since the Industrial Revolution, which began in the late eighteenth century in England. Scientists say carbon

Tugboats pull the crippled tanker Exxon Valdez *in Alaska's Prince William Sound in April 1989.*

levels are the highest they have been in known history. Excess carbon dioxide in the atmosphere poses important environmental risks that scientists are looking at more and more. Some scientists believe elevated levels of carbon dioxide in the atmosphere will allow less heat to escape. This could warm the earth.

Until recently, the United States was the leading source of carbon dioxide in the world. Now, the United States is second only to China. Environmentalists and politicians are working to reduce carbon emissions in the United States and have seen some success. A *New York Times* report from the U.S. Department of Energy notes, "Emissions of carbon dioxide from fuel burned in the United States dropped 1.3 percent in 2006 compared with an all-time peak reached the year before."[1] The *Times* reports, however, that the lower emissions may be more the result of the high cost of fuel than political efforts to control emissions.

Smog

Exhaust from cars, factories, and power plants combines in the air to form a toxic mix of gaseous chemicals called smog. Smog consists primarily of carbon monoxide, nitrogen dioxide, sulfur dioxide, and ozone. Smog is often a problem in cities, especially in California. Health risks such as asthma, bronchitis, and emphysema can be exacerbated by smog.

CLIMATE CHANGE

Scientists predict that elevated levels of carbon dioxide in the atmosphere could have a severe effect on global climate. Others oppose the idea of human-induced global warming. "There is no debate among any statured scientists working on this issue about the larger trends in what is happening to the climate," says James McCarthy of the United Nations Intergovernmental Panel on Climate Change.[2] These scientists agree that the earth is experiencing an unnatural warming due to an excess of greenhouse gases, such as carbon dioxide, and have observed its effects across the globe.

Meteorologists and other scientists who study the effects of climate change have noted an increase in temperatures worldwide. Scientists believe this increase is responsible for the extreme weather conditions many parts of the globe have experienced in recent years. Increased temperatures are most extreme at the North Pole and the South Pole, where scientists have observed greater than usual ice melt. This melting means that the ice caps are shrinking. Sea levels could rise dramatically

Al Gore and Global Warming

Since the end of his term as U.S. vice president in January 2001, Al Gore has become an important figure in the global-warming debate. Gore has pushed for legislation that would reduce the amount of carbon dioxide emissions in the United States. He also lectures widely on the topic to promote awareness of the "climate crisis."

In 2006, Gore's lectures on climate change were adapted into the feature film *An Inconvenient Truth*. The film prompted worldwide interest and increased awareness of climate change. Gore states in the film, "We are witnessing an unprecedented and massive collision between our civilization and the Earth."[3] The film won an Academy Award for Best Documentary Feature.

In 2007, Gore was awarded the Nobel Peace Price, which he shares with the Intergovernmental Panel on Climate Change, "for their efforts to build up and disseminate greater knowledge about man-made climate change, and to lay the foundations for the measures that are needed to counteract such change."[4]

Global Warming Myth

Some politicians and citizens oppose the theory of human-induced global warming. They doubt that human activity could have such a drastic effect in so short a time. Earth is known to have gone through natural periods of warming and cooling, and it is possible that the planet is going through a natural warming period.

if the melting continues. According to Al Gore, former vice president of the United States and environmentalist, "If Greenland melted or broke up and slipped into the sea . . . sea levels worldwide would increase between 18 and 20 feet."[5] Gore goes on to note that this rise in sea level would flood low-lying lands and reshape many important cities. The shrinking ice caps have also put wildlife such as polar bears, penguins, and seals at risk of extinction because their habitat is being compromised.

Global warming has become an important issue to many people. Because scientists believe global warming correlates strongly to carbon dioxide levels, it has become more important to find ways to reduce carbon emissions. One way to do this is by conserving energy. For example, people can make sure appliances are not running unnecessarily and use appliances that are energy efficient. People can also reduce carbon emissions through the use of alternative fuels.

Al Gore, former U.S. vice president, was awarded the 2007 Nobel Peace Prize for his efforts to educate the world about climate change.

A train with spent nuclear fuel passes the cooling towers as it leaves a nuclear power plant in Germany in 2001. The train is headed for a nuclear reprocessing plant in western France.

CARBON-FREE ENERGY

*I*ndustries and governments are considering a variety of energy alternatives that could offset dependence on crude oil. The "Go Green!" initiative in the United States has many citizens encouraged by the more widespread availability of energy alternatives to crude oil. Some of these resources have the added benefit of being able to produce energy without producing carbon dioxide. Many of these alternative energy sources are being used today and may be used more frequently in the near future.

NUCLEAR POWER

Nuclear power was introduced to the United States in 1957. Typically, nuclear power is made using uranium, which is a radioactive metal. In a controlled process called nuclear fission, nuclei of uranium atoms are split. When this happens, a large amount of energy is released as heat. Nuclear fission must be highly controlled to ensure that the process does not happen too quickly. This would release more heat than the reactor in the power plant can handle.

Nuclear power plants gained popularity in the United States during the 1960s and 1970s. Popularity waned when accidents occurred at Three Mile Island in Pennsylvania in 1979 and Chernobyl in Ukraine in 1986. New construction of nuclear

U.S. Energy Consumption

According to the U.S. Energy Information Administration, U.S. energy consumption by energy source in 2005 was approximately:

- Petroleum: 40 percent
- Natural gas: 23 percent
- Coal: 23 percent
- Nuclear: 8 percent
- Renewable: 7 percent

power plants in the United States came to a halt. In 2005, according to the U.S. Energy Information Administration, nuclear energy provided the United States with 8 percent of its total energy consumption.

As a carbon-free energy source, nuclear power is gaining attention from some environmentalists. Patrick Moore, one of the cofounders of Greenpeace, was a staunch opponent of nuclear power in the 1970s. However, Moore now appreciates how valuable nuclear power is as

Three Mile Island

In 1979, an accident occurred at the Three Mile Island nuclear power facility in Pennsylvania. A maintenance error and defective valve caused the nuclear reactor to overheat. The system automatically began to run its cooling system, but it was turned off by a plant worker in error. Turning off the cooling system caused the nuclear core, where nuclear reactions occur, to create energy and melt. The nuclear core was severely damaged.

The accident caused a small amount of radioactive gas to be released, putting the public at risk of exposure. However, most scientists agree that public health was not put at significant risk. Still, the public became increasingly concerned about the risks of nuclear power. Following the accident, additional safety measures were required on new nuclear power facilities in the United States. These measures significantly increased costs of constructing nuclear power plants. Several construction projects were abandoned because of the new standards.

The presence of nuclear power in the United States has dwindled since the 1970s. No new nuclear power plants have been built in the United States since 1974. The accident at Three Mile Island is largely judged to be the result of human error, though there are arguments for a design issue.

a carbon-free energy source:

> *My views have changed, and the rest of the environmental movement needs to update its views, too, because nuclear energy may just be the energy source that can save our planet from another possible disaster: catastrophic climate change.*[1]

Still, even supporters such as Moore recognize the difficulty in convincing the public to turn to nuclear energy. Nuclear power is still perceived as dangerous, from its creation to the disposal of nuclear waste. There is also fear of nuclear plants being targeted by terrorists.

Solar Power

Earth's main source of energy is the sun. It heats the planet and provides plant life with energy. The amount of solar energy that reaches the earth's surface varies due to time of day, cloud cover, and other weather conditions. Still, the sun constantly shines on the planet. Sunlight is the earth's most constant renewable source of energy. It is also carbon-free. Solar

A Million Solar Roofs

On August 21, 2006, California Governor Arnold Schwarzenegger signed a bill authorizing the Million Solar Roofs plan. California will work toward building 1 million solar roofs by the year 2017. Because of the amount of sunlight in California each day, the state has a huge potential to make solar energy a valuable energy source.

power has been in use since the 1950s but has not gained widespread use. Solar power plants do not produce as much power as traditional power plants, and installing solar panels on individual homes can be expensive. In addition, solar energy does not run once the sun has set. Methods for storing solar energy, such as solar-thermal plants, must be created. Still, the use of solar cells is growing. Some cities use solar cells to power outdoor lighting and parking meters. With the increased interest in alternative energy sources, it is hoped that solar technology can be improved so that it becomes more efficient and less expensive.

Wind Power

The U.S. Energy Information Administration

Windmills and Birds

Despite attempts to help the environment by using renewable energy sources, there can be negative effects as well. According to a 2003 report by the National Renewable Energy Laboratory, windmills in California's Altamont Pass kill approximately 1,000 birds each year.

reports that wind energy accounted for approximately 3 percent of all U.S. energy consumed in 2005. Wind power is emissions-free, renewable, and also occurs naturally. Windmills, or turbines, can send energy to local buildings or charge batteries that can be used later.

White Bluffs Solar Station near Richland, Washington, is near the abandoned Washington Nuclear Project One.

Dozens of U.S. states have the ability to harness the wind for power. Texas, California, Minnesota, Iowa, and Washington have the greatest wind power capacity. Location is important in building wind farms because some areas are consistently less windy than others—wind farms are not always a good alternate energy source. They must be far from buildings, trees, or other things that could block the wind. Wind farms are often built in coastal regions or at sea. Like solar energy, storage methods for wind power are needed.

HYDROGEN FUEL

Hydrogen is the most common element in the universe. It is readily available on Earth, and it carries energy. Scientists have learned to use hydrogen to produce fuel. However, this new technology is not yet ready for commercial applications.

As a fuel, hydrogen could be used to run certain types of automobiles. Instead of exhaust fumes, hydrogen-run cars would emit water. Hydrogen fuel cells allow hydrogen and oxygen to combine, producing water and electricity. Because hydrogen fuel is carbon-free, it is gaining popularity.

On Earth, hydrogen typically bonds with, or attaches to, other elements. In order to produce hydrogen fuel, scientists must break those bonds—the hydrogen must remain unattached. Doing so requires a good deal of energy, and fossil fuels are typically used to aid this process. If hydrogen fuel is produced commercially, transitioning to solar or wind power could make the entire process carbon-free. ⌐

A pair of wind turbines dwarfs a farmstead in Kansas. The wind farm's 170 turbines can generate enough electricity to power 40,000 households.

A nuclear power plant and an adjacent experimental solar field

ARGUMENTS SUPPORTING ALTERNATIVE ENERGY USE

*D*espite challenges that alternative energy sources present, they remain desirable technologies. Carbon-free energy sources may not yet be ready for large-scale implementation, but investment in these technologies could make them viable options in the near future. Nuclear, solar, wind, and hydrogen powers all have benefits. One or more of these energy sources could be the next big U.S. industry, helping to reduce U.S. dependence on oil.

NUCLEAR ENERGY IS A PROVEN TECHNOLOGY

Nuclear power could drastically reduce carbon emissions. As an alternative energy source, it is perhaps the most advanced and easiest technology to incorporate into the current U.S. energy infrastructure.

Nuclear power provides the world with one-sixth of its electricity. "Current technology is capable of providing lower cost, safe energy in virtually infinite amounts," says engineer and nuclear power advocate Tom Solon.[1] It is efficient and produces vast amounts of energy. In addition, nuclear plants require only a fraction of the space that solar power plants or wind farms require.

Carbon Footprint

A carbon footprint is the measure of human impact on the environment by measure of carbon emissions. It is not only a measure of an individual's impact. A carbon footprint can also measure the effect of an organization, product, or service on the environment. It accounts for electricity use, transportation, and consumption of products that use fossil fuels in production. Knowledge of the activities that contribute to carbon emissions helps individuals reduce their carbon footprints.

Hydrogen Cars

Most major automobile manufacturers are developing vehicles that will run on hydrogen. Several prototypes have been made, and a few are already on the roads. In California, approximately 200 hydrogen-run vehicles were on the road as of early 2007.

Nuclear power reduces dependency on oil. After the 1973 oil crunch, Japan expanded its nuclear industry. In 1990, Japan relied on oil for 58 percent of its energy. That figure dropped to 52 percent in 2000. Almost one-third of Japan's electricity comes from nuclear power.

WIDE-SCALE USE WILL LOWER COSTS

Advocates of alternative energies such as solar, wind, and hydrogen argue that these technologies would become more efficient and less expensive if they were used more widely. Manufacturing costs would decrease, and demand for improved technologies would increase.

According to Glenn Hammer of the Solar Energy Industries Association, the photovoltaics (solar energy cells) industry has seen significant growth. As large orders are placed, the cost has come down. In 2004, solar energy cost $7 to $10 per watt. By 2010, prices are expected to come down to $3 or $4 per watt. Photovoltaics have experienced technological improvements. More energy can be produced from photovoltaics today than those of the same size in the 1990s.

Wind energy is experiencing similar growth. Approximately 6,000 megawatts of wind capacity are added each year to power 1.5 million homes. The cost of wind power is also dropping. It fell from 12¢ per kilowatt-hour in 1985 to 5¢ per kilowatt-hour in 2005.

Federal tax credits for alternative energy industries are reducing costs and prompting growth in those industries. Industrial growth encourages investment. With this funding,

Kyoto Protocol

The Kyoto Protocol is an international treaty designed to reduce the amount of greenhouse gases linked to global warming. These gases include carbon dioxide, methane, nitrous oxide, hydrofluorocarbons, perfluorocarbons, and sulfur hexafluoride. This United Nations treaty was agreed upon in 1997 and went into effect in February 2005.

Developed nations participating in the treaty determine their individual national policies to reduce their emissions. Countries are allowed to offset their emissions by reforestation, or increasing vegetation, to comply with a portion of their reduced emissions goals. Countries are expected to start achieving these reforestation goals by 2008, and all target goals are to be reached by 2012.

The United States failed to ratify the Kyoto Protocol. Although the United States initially supported the treaty under President Bill Clinton, it was not presented to Congress during his term in office. President George W. Bush opposed the treaty because it does not require developing nations to reduce emissions. Australia did not initially sign the treaty but ratified the Kyoto Protocol in late 2007.

Types of Solar Power

There are three main types of solar energy:
• Photovoltaics convert energy from the sun into electricity.
• Concentrating solar power converts heat from the sun into electricity by means of steam.
• Solar thermal uses sunlight to heat buildings and water. Solar thermal does not create electricity.

technological advancements can be made that will make these energies more viable. Engineers in these industries predict substantial growth in the coming years due, in part, to extra funding for research.

More Jobs

Increased demand for alternative energies increases demand for workers to make these technologies available. Investments in alternative energies jumped from $623 million in 2005 to $1.5 billion in 2006. New alternative energy companies are creating jobs in the industry. In Toledo, Ohio, 6,000 people are employed in the solar power industry. These jobs range from engineers and chemists to marketing directors, secretaries, and mechanics. If growth in the solar energy industry continues at its current rate, there could be 150,000 jobs by 2020. ⌐

In February 2008, the Ningde Nuclear Power Plant in southeast China was under construction. The first of four reactors is expected to begin commercial use at the end of 2012.

Many people are opposed to nuclear energy, including the activists who marched in Rennes, France, on March 17, 2007. Their banner reads, "Yes to alternative solution against nuclear."

ARGUMENTS AGAINST
ALTERNATIVE ENERGY USE

lternative energy sources are gaining
more attention worldwide. Although
many Americans are attracted to the idea of
alternative energy, many economists and scientists

point out that the alternatives are still inefficient sources of energy when compared to oil. As U.S. Vice President Dick Cheney said in 2001, "Conservation may be a sign of personal virtue, but it is not a sufficient basis, all by itself, for a sound, comprehensive energy policy."[1]

Changing the entire U.S. energy infrastructure will be a massive undertaking that the country simply may not be ready for. The technology behind many alternatives will have to be significantly improved if they are to be implemented on a large scale.

Oil Is Inexpensive and Efficient

Despite increasing prices, oil is still the most inexpensive source of energy. As long as oil is available at a cost lesser than alternative energy sources, it will not make financial

First Fuel Cells

British physicist Sir William Robert Grove invented the first hydrogen fuel cell in 1839. Grove first ran an electric current through water to split it into hydrogen and oxygen. He then combined hydrogen and oxygen, creating electrical energy. At the time, Grove noted that the process could have applications for replacing coal and wood as energy sources.

sense to change the current energy system in the United States. The market does not take the so-called "cost" of carbon emissions into consideration. Therefore, there will not be a meaningful demand for an alternative to oil as long as cheap oil is widely available. According to Ali al-Naimi, Saudi Arabia's minister of oil and mineral resources, "Oil will still dominate for the next 30–50 years, because there are no meaningful substitutes."[2]

Alternatives such as solar and wind power plants are costly to implement. Solar cells are expensive and cannot compete with traditional energy. Journalist Michael Fox has reported many failed solar and wind power projects. The solar power tower in California is reported to have consumed more energy than it produced.

In addition to the initial installation costs, some alternative energies have maintenance costs. Also, solar and wind energies' dependence on weather conditions makes them unreliable and less effective than oil. And because power plants that run on fossil fuels operate despite weather conditions, even when solar and wind sources are incorporated into the current energy infrastructure, they are not reported to significantly reduce carbon emissions.

Nuclear Power Is Too Risky

Despite the numerous safety regulations nuclear power plants must meet, many people still consider nuclear power dangerous. If it is not properly controlled, an accident could release radioactive gas or radiation into the environment. This could harm public health. Some types of radiation have been linked to genetic disorders and cancer.

Nuclear waste is also an issue. Each of the 103 nuclear reactors in the United States produces approximately 3,000 tons (2,700 t) of radioactive waste a year. Approximately 88,000 tons (80,000 t) of nuclear waste is sitting in cooling pools waiting for the U.S. government to determine how to dispose of it. The Yucca Mountain Repository in Nevada was scheduled to open in 1998, but construction problems and public

Chernobyl

On April 26, 1986, an accident at the Chernobyl nuclear power facility in Ukraine caused an explosion that sent radioactive debris into the air. The debris reached the western Soviet Union, Eastern Europe, and Scandinavia. Containment of the radiation was made worse because firefighters used water to put out a fire, sending radioactive steam into the air.

Farmland was removed from production, and an increase in thyroid cancer was observed in children where there were high levels of radiation. The number of human deaths caused by the Chernobyl disaster is difficult to estimate because "radiation" is not always listed as the cause of death. However, a 2005 study attributes approximately 50 deaths directly to the accident. Additional deaths due to cancer caused by radiation could eventually surpass 4,000. The Chernobyl explosion is the worst nuclear power accident in history.

opposition have slowed the process. Citizens want promises that waste will not leak. Engineers cannot yet make such promises.

Meanwhile, thousands of tons of radioactive waste await disposal. In 2005, the National Academy of Sciences released a study showing that cooling pools are more vulnerable to terrorist attacks than federal regulators want to admit. These pools store 10 to 30 times more radioactive material than is housed in a nuclear reactor. An attack on these sites could release immense

Yucca Mountain

The Yucca Mountain in Nevada is located approximately 100 miles (161 km) northwest of Las Vegas. This volcanic mountain was chosen by the U.S. government in 1987 as the first permanent underground repository for nuclear waste. The Yucca Mountain Repository is limited by federal law to 77,162 tons (70,000 t) of waste. As of 2002, approximately 61,729 tons (56,000 t) of waste are waiting to be disposed of at the repository.

Opposition to the site has delayed the repository's completion. State officials are concerned that the waste could leak from the storage containers because minerals in the mountain are able to erode the proposed containers.

In addition, some geological studies have indicated that the site is unfit for long-term containment of nuclear waste. The mountain's volcanic rock is porous and would not be able to contain radiation should containers break. Also, the area is prone to earthquakes. Geologists have counted 32 earthquake faults, leading them to believe the mountain could be unstable and unsuitable as a waste site.

As of 2005, the U.S. government has spent $6 billion on developing the Yucca Mountain Repository. It expects to spend another $50 billion on construction and operation of the facility. The site is expected to be completed in 2010.

amounts of radiation into the environment, which could harm wildlife and human health.

HYDROGEN TECHNOLOGY IS NOT READY

Although hydrogen fuel cells have been in development for years, they are not advanced enough to sufficiently power an automobile. Some hydrogen-run prototypes are in development, but most automobile-industry executives admit the prototypes are nowhere near ready for mass production. Bill Reinert, national manager for Toyota's advanced technology group, says:

> *High-volume production could be 25 years off. I'm less than hopeful about reducing costs sufficiently, and I'm quite pessimistic about solving hydrogen storage issues and packaging these large systems in a marketable vehicle.*[3]

While fuel cells operate effectively in laboratory settings, placement in automobiles poses problems. A variety of technical issues will have to be resolved before hydrogen fuel can become

NASA

Chemists at General Flectric Company developed the first commercial fuel cell in the 1950s. NASA picked up the technology and first used it in the 1960s during the Gemini space program. The water produced from fuel cells is so pure that astronauts drink it in space during shuttle missions.

Powering Hydrogen

A good deal of energy is needed to create hydrogen fuel cells. In many cases, fossil fuels are burned to create this energy. Environmentalists suggest that solar or wind power could one day replace fossil fuels in the hydrogen-power process. However, given the amount of energy required to produce hydrogen power, the United States would need an enormous solar plant or wind farm to support a hydrogen economy.

a viable alternative fuel source. For example, fuel cells must be perfected to perform in hot and cold weather, storage in tanks must be made safe, and fuel must be readily available.

One of the biggest hurdles for the automotive industry will be implementing a hydrogen infrastructure. Consumers will not be willing to purchase cars if they cannot refuel easily. With a limited number of hydrogen vehicles on the road, fuel stations may not be willing to add hydrogen fuel pumps. Whether or not hydrogen will become an effective fuel alternative is still unknown. Right now, the technology is still a long way off.

Tunnels are being constructed at Yucca Mountain, where the U.S. government plans to create the world's first high-level radioactive waste dump.

A section of land inside the Arctic National Wildlife Refuge in Alaska

Solutions That Bridge the Gap

Although carbon-free energy would be the most efficient way for Americans to reduce their carbon emissions, many are doubtful that the United States could fully transition to those energy sources. Fossil fuels are a big part of the

American lifestyle, and alternative energy sources are not yet able to meet U.S. energy needs. It will take decades to fully transition. According to Michael D. Lemonick, a reporter for *Time* magazine:

> As consumers, we need time to make adjustments—often very expensive ones—to the new technologies. . . . And although energy and power companies are investing in new technologies, they can't create a massive new infrastructure overnight.[1]

In the meantime, politicians and economists champion other ideas that would reduce U.S. dependence on foreign oil. By increasing U.S. reserves and decreasing consumption, many hope the United States could become energy independent in a shorter period of time. Even with continued oil use, innovative fuel technologies can offset current carbon dioxide emissions rates. Although the effects on the environment would not be as significant as carbon-free fuels, environmentalists believe the effects of reduced emissions could be substantial.

"Our ignorance is not so vast as our failure to use what we know."[2]

—M. King Hubbert, geophysicist

DRILLING IN ALASKA

A new area for oil exploration is the Arctic
Circle. Canada, Denmark, Greenland, Norway,
Russia, and the United States are among the
countries looking to the Arctic for new sources
of oil. At the Arctic Energy Summit in October
2007, Brenda Pierce of the U.S. Geological Survey
explained that the Arctic could hold 14 percent of
the world's undiscovered oil and natural gas reserves.
Pierce notes that "14 percent could understate
the Arctic's potential."[3] Furthermore, the East
Siberian basin could hold an additional 11 percent of
undiscovered oil and natural gas reserves.

With oil prices on the rise, these countries are
taking a greater interest in exploring this region
for oil. Arctic melting due to climate change is also
making exploration and drilling in the Arctic easier
for oil companies.

Arctic drilling in the United States would take
place in Alaska. The Arctic National Wildlife Refuge
(ANWR) is located in northeastern Alaska on the
North Slope. In 1960, ANWR was designated as a
conservation area. Originally 8.9 million acres (3.6
million ha), as of 2007, ANWR now comprises
approximately 19 million acres (7.7 million ha)

of land. It is the nation's largest wildlife refuge.

ANWR is home to dozens of species of land animals, including moose, musk oxen, and polar bears. It is also an important migratory destination for millions of birds and thousands of caribou. The caribou attract predators such as grizzly bears and wolves to the region.

Only the U.S. Congress can approve drilling in ANWR. Studies of the environmental impact of drilling in ANWR are inconclusive. Oil rigs at Alaska's Prudhoe Bay, just north of ANWR, appear to have not affected the population of caribou in that area. However, some environmentalists argue that the presence of oil rigs and pipelines in ANWR could disrupt the migratory patterns and birthing of caribou. Environmentalists oppose drilling in ANWR because it could adversely

Aboriginal People in Alaska

The Inupiat Eskimos live on the north shore of Alaska and are permitted to hunt and fish in ANWR. Many Inupiat have benefited from the oil industry in Prudhoe Bay and support drilling in ANWR.

The Gwich'in Athabascan Indians live on the southern border of ANWR. They depend on the caribou to support their way of life and oppose drilling in ANWR.

affect some species at risk of endangerment.
According to Greenpeace:

> *Arctic wildlife is already gravely threatened by global*
> *warming, caused by the very industries that are lobbying to*
> *open up this wildlife haven. Polar bears, caribou, migratory*
> *birds and other animals would be exposed to the inevitable oil*
> *spills and pollution if development is approved.*
>
> *Drilling in our protected lands is not the solution to our*
> *energy crisis. Everyone agrees we should be striving for energy*
> *independence, but the best way to achieve that is through*
> *investing our tax dollars in clean, renewable energy such as*
> *solar and wind.*[4]

Still, large amounts of oil are expected to be
found in ANWR. Drilling would be done in a small
portion of the reserve, comprising 2,000 acres (809
ha). The Prudhoe Bay oil field is located in ANWR.
Researcher Mac Johnson notes:

> *While Prudhoe Bay produces an impressive 400,000 barrels*
> *per day, the Energy Information Agency estimates that peak*
> *production from ANWR would likely be 900,000 barrels*
> *per day—an incredible 222 percent of Prudhoe Bay.*[5]

Alaska is estimated to hold more oil than any other
region in the United States.

Oil extracted from ANWR could greatly reduce U.S. dependence on foreign oil. Still, drilling in ANWR will not solve the problem of carbon emissions and climate change. Charles Krauthammer of the *Washington Post* writes:

> *No one pretends that this fixes everything. But a million barrels a day from the Arctic National Wildlife Refuge is 5 percent of our consumption. In tight markets, that makes a crucial difference.* [6]

HYBRID ELECTRIC VEHICLES

While oil continues to be the main source of energy in the United States, researchers are developing methods to reduce emissions. One popular example is the hybrid electric vehicle (HEV). HEVs use a combination of an internal combustion engine and an electric battery that power an electric motor to power the vehicle. Many HEVs charge the electric battery through kinetic energy from braking or from the

Toyota Prius

The Toyota Prius hybrid vehicle was first sold in Japan in 1997. The Prius went worldwide in 2001. The 2007 model has been estimated by the EPA to get 46 miles per gallon (20 km/L). It has won several awards and is easily recognized for its aerodynamic design. The Prius is the most popular hybrid vehicle sold to date.

internal combustion engine, which shuts down when the vehicle is idling for more economical fuel consumption.

Hybrid vehicles were first introduced to the United States in 1999 with the Honda Insight. Other hybrid vehicles have followed, including the Toyota Prius, the Honda Civic Hybrid, and the Ford Escape Hybrid. Many car manufacturers now have hybrid versions of their popular models on the roads or in development. According to *Time* magazine's Michael D. Lemonick:

> *The frenzy to churn out hybrids and their technological cousins is so fierce that archrivals GM, DaimlerChrysler and BMW have teamed up to build a research and technical center in the Detroit suburbs.*[7]

Hybrid vehicles consume approximately half the amount of fuel of those run solely on internal combustion engines. This reduces energy consumption

The Popularity of HEVs

HEVs are popular because owners can see the effects of their purchases immediately in their daily gas use. In addition, HEVs purchased by U.S. citizens are also eligible for a tax break. Toyota is the leader in hybrid vehicles. In 2006, Toyota reported that worldwide sales of HEVs exceeded 500,000. Of that, 250,000 HEVs were sold in the United States.

Of the 500,000 HEVs sold by Toyota in 2006, half were sold in the United States. The Toyota Prius is the top selling hybrid in the United States.

and carbon emissions. Norma Carr–Ruffino and John Acheson report for the *Futurist*:

> *Hybrids have saved more than an estimated one million barrels of crude oil, three million pounds of smog–forming gases, one million metric tons of carbon dioxide and an estimated 125 million gallons of gasoline.*[8]

Opponents argue that fuel economy, whether through hybrid vehicles or higher Corporate Average Fuel Economy standards, will do little for the environment. When car owners are not required to spend as much on gas, they will travel more, which will increase fuel consumption. Therefore, improved efficiency is not an answer to U.S. dependence on oil. Instead, they argue, carbon-free technologies need to be implemented.

Still, hybrids may be able to help reduce dependence on oil. According to Carr-Ruffino and Acheson:

> *Benefits of hybrid technologies go well beyond gas mileage and saving money. They lead toward new applications and platforms. The hybrid has the potential to lead to greater innovations for a growing number of products and services.* [9]

Hybrid technology could pave the way for smoother implementation of hydrogen technology.

Biodiesel

The development of biodiesel was important in the search for renewable fuels. Biodiesel can be used to run unmodified diesel vehicles. Diesel engines are used in factories, power generators, construction vehicles, and commercial trucks.

BIOFUELS

The U.S. government promotes use of biofuels such as biodiesel and ethanol. Biofuels are renewable fuels made from biological matter. They emit less carbon dioxide than gas. Biofuel use also offsets their carbon emissions because plants absorb carbon dioxide.

Biodiesel is derived from canola, soy, or palm oil. Ethanol is a type of alcohol scientists use to make fuel. Ethanol is the most popular biofuel in the United States. Typically, ethanol is made from corn in the United States. It also can be made from many other plants, including sugarcane, switch grass, or poplar. Ethanol fuel is generally made by blending ethanol with gasoline. In 2006, U.S. biorefineries converted approximately 20 percent of the U.S. corn crop into ethanol. This number increased to 27 percent in 2007. That

Biomass Energy

Energy derived from biological material is referred to as biomass energy. This type of energy can be made from plants, wood, and dung. Waste from crops and sewage can be converted into energy through chemical processes. Biomass also includes biofuels such as ethanol and biodiesel.

Biomass energy is the most widely used renewable energy source in the United States. According to the U.S. Energy Information Administration, biomass energy accounted for 50 percent of the renewable energy consumed in the United States in 2005. It also accounted for 4 percent of total energy consumed.

Environmentalists are intrigued by the idea of expanding the use of biomass energy. For them, it solves the problems of both waste and energy. By using organic materials that otherwise would have gone to landfills for fuel, the United States could potentially have an endless supply of energy. Still, there are environmental issues. Although biofuels do not have as significant an impact on the environment as petroleum, burning biofuels produces pollution. In addition, some are concerned about the impact of using land to grow crops for energy.

percentage is expected to increase further. The number of biorefineries is growing as well. As of October 2007, 114 were in operation, with 80 more under construction.

President George W. Bush has pushed for more ethanol to be produced in the United States as an alternative fuel. Under President Bush's plan, the United States should be producing 35 billion gallons (132 billion L) of ethanol by 2017. John Coequyt, on behalf of Greenpeace, said in response, "An aggressive focus on ethanol, without a federally mandated cap on emissions, is simply a leap sideways."[10]

Using biofuels such as ethanol reduces emissions. But reduction may not be enough. Fossil fuels are used to produce and transport ethanol. Some estimates say this use of fossil fuels negates saved emissions that using biofuels would bring.

In addition, in order to meet President Bush's target for ethanol production, the entire U.S. corn crop would need to be dedicated to ethanol production. Although the United States currently has a surplus of corn, using it to produce ethanol would negatively affect its use in food products. Widespread use of ethanol also carries the risks

Corn is dumped at an ethanol-manufacturing facility in Indiana. As the popularity of ethanol increases, corn will go to such facilities rather than to food manufacturers.

associated with solar and wind power—its availability is dependent on weather conditions. A severe drought could greatly limit access to ethanol. In this event, the United States could purchase ethanol from other countries. For example, Brazil has become a major producer of ethanol developed from sugarcane. However, this would leave the problem of dependency on foreign nations for energy unsolved.

Ethanol, HEVs, and drilling in ANWR have their benefits. These alternative energy sources are a step in reducing both U.S. dependence on foreign oil and the amount of carbon emissions. Some analysts contend that these goals are unnecessary and not truly beneficial to the U.S. economy. Still, many individuals, organizations, and governments are becoming mindful of the potential effects of oil consumption on the world. Some are taking steps to change their energy use, which includes the pursuit of alternative resources. But the process is slow. Until alternative energy sources can be fully incorporated into the U.S. infrastructure, such sacrifices as dependence on foreign oil, decreased corn for food, and drilling of protected wilderness lands may be the only options.

Wind turbines churn out electricity in the distance as a pump pulls oil from the ground

TIMELINE

1956	1960	1960
Geophysicist M. King Hubbert predicts that U.S. oil production will peak between 1965 and 1970.	The Organization of the Petroleum Exporting Countries (OPEC) is founded.	The Arctic National Wildlife Refuge is designated a conservation area.

146th OPEC Conference December 2007, Abu Dhabi,

1977	1979	1980
President Jimmy Carter warns of the dangers of excess oil consumption and calls for oil conservation.	The Three Mile Island nuclear reactor melts down.	The United States supports Iraq in the Iran-Iraq War (1980–1988).

1971

Oil production in the United States peaks.

1973

An oil crisis occurs in the United States when OPEC tightens output during the Arab-Israeli War.

1975

U.S. Congress enacts Corporate Average Fuel Economy standards.

1986

An explosion at the Chernobyl nuclear power facility sends radioactive material across the countryside and into other countries.

1988

Yucca Mountain in Nevada is designated a nuclear repository site.

1989

The *Exxon Valdez* oil tanker runs aground on March 24, spilling 11 million gallons of crude oil.

TIMELINE

1990	1991	1995
Iraq invades Kuwait on August 2.	President George H. W. Bush launches Operation Desert Storm on January 17.	The UN establishes a food-for-oil program in Iraq.

2005	2005	2005
The international Kyoto Protocol treaty to reduce carbon emissions goes into effect in February.	On August 8, President George W. Bush signs the Energy Policy Act, the nation's first national energy plan in ten years.	Hurricanes Katrina and Rita hit the Gulf Coast of the United States, damaging refineries.

1999

The Honda Insight is the first hybrid vehicle sold in the United States.

2001

Terrorists, including many Saudi nationals, attack the United States on September 11, prompting belief that Saudi oil sales fund terrorism.

2003

The United States invades Iraq on March 19.

2006

An Inconvenient Truth is released in theaters, increasing public concern about climate change.

2007

The Toyota Prius is the most popular hybrid car sold to date.

2008

The price of gas surpasses $4.00 per gallon in the spring.

ESSENTIAL FACTS

AT ISSUE

Arguments For an Oil Crisis

❖ Oil is a finite resource, and it is running out.

❖ The United States should reduce the use of fossil fuels.

❖ The United States should use renewable resources.

Arguments Against an Oil Crisis

❖ Oil is plentiful.

❖ The United States should increase its production of crude oil.

❖ Renewable energy sources are not feasible.

CRITICAL DATES

1956
M. King Hubbert presented his peak oil theory. Because oil is a nonrenewable resource, production will peak and then begin to decline. Hubbert predicted that oil production in the United States would peak between 1965 and 1970 and world oil production would peak in 2000.

1973
An oil crisis occurred in the United States when OPEC tightened output during the Arab-Israeli War. Fuel was in short supply and prices increased dramatically, making fuel difficult for many Americans to afford.

1999
The Honda Insight hybrid vehicle began to be sold in the United States. Other hybrid vehicles became available soon after.

2001

On September 11, terrorists attacked New York City and Washington DC. Many of the terrorists were Saudi nationals. The American media began to speculate that the revenues from oil purchased from Saudi Arabia funded terrorist activity.

2005

Hurricanes Katrina and Rita struck the Gulf Coast of the United States in the fall, damaging oil refineries and reducing fuel production. The price of fuel jumped significantly in response to the limited supply, and the price of oil became a matter of national interest.

2006

The film *An Inconvenient Truth* was released in theaters. Public concern about climate change and carbon dioxide emissions increased in response.

Quotes

"When the market is running tight, anything—whether it's a hurricane, or war, or revolution, or terrorism—can precipitate a crisis."—*Robert J. Lieber*

"Fuels recede, demand grows, efficiency makes things worse . . . it will all run out but we will always find more."—*Peter W. Huber and Mark P. Mills,* The Bottomless Well

ADDITIONAL RESOURCES

SELECT BIBLIOGRAPHY

Gore, Al. *An Inconvenient Truth*. Emmaus, PA: Rodale, 2006.

Huber, Peter W. and Mark P. Mills, *The Bottomless Well*. New York: Basic Books, 2005.

Klare, Michael T. *Blood and Oil*. New York: Metropolitan Books, 2004.

"Oil (Petroleum) and Gasoline." Times Topics. *New York Times* 7 Nov. 2007 <http://topics.nytimes.com/top/reference/timestopics/subjects/o/oil_petroleum_and_gasoline/index.html>.

FURTHER READING

Allaby, Michael. *Fog, Smog, and Poisoned Rain*. New York: Facts on File, 2003.

Kort, Michael. *Handbook of the Middle East*. New York: Twentieth Century Books, 2007.

Nakaya, Andrea C. Ed. *Oil*. Detroit, MI: Thomson Gale, 2006.

Passero, Barbara. Ed. *Energy Alternatives*. Detroit, MI: Thomson Gale, 2006.

WEB LINKS

To learn more about oil and energy alternatives, visit ABDO Publishing Company on the World Wide Web at **www.abdopublishing.com**. Web sites about oil and energy alternatives are featured on our Book Links page. These links are routinely monitored and updated to provide the most current information available.

For More Information

For more information on this subject, contact or visit the following organizations.

American Petroleum Institute
1220 L Street Northwest, Washington DC 20005
202-682-8000
www.api.org
The American Petroleum Institute represents the oil and natural gas industry in the United States. The organization compiles research and statistics, and speaks on behalf of the oil industry.

Greenpeace
702 H Street, Northwest, Washington DC 20001
202-462-1177
www.greenpeace.org
Greenpeace is an organization that advocates protecting wildlife and environmental conservation. It supports the use of carbon-free energy.

Renewable Fuel Association
1 Massachusetts Avenue Northwest, Suite 820, Washington DC 20001
202-289-3835
www.ethanolrfa.org
The Renewable Fuel Association supports the ethanol industry by promoting research and development of ethanol as a fuel alternative. It also provides data to the media and to government agencies.

GLOSSARY

biodiesel
> A type of biofuel made from canola, soy, or palm oil that can be used to run diesel engines.

biofuel
> Any fuel made from or consisting of organic material.

carbon dioxide
> A gas composed of the elements carbon and oxygen; people exhale it and burning fossil fuels releases it.

climate change
> A measurable increase or decrease in average temperatures across the globe.

economic
> Pertaining to how consumers spend their money and the effects this has on manufacturing and services.

efficiency
> The ability to do something without excess waste.

emission
> The release of something, such as gas or chemicals, into the air.

ethanol
> A type of alcohol produced from plants such as corn, sugarcane, switch grass, and poplar that has been used to create fuel.

finite
> Having a limited supply.

greenhouse gas
> Gases that help hold heat in Earth's atmosphere.

hybrid electric vehicle
> A vehicle that is powered by a combination of traditional fuel and electricity.

hydrogen fuel cell
> A device that uses electricity to produce fuel from hydrogen.

import
> To bring something from another country for sale.

industrialization
> The development of businesses and factories in a country or a region.

infrastructure
> The structures and facilities needed to run a system or a society.

meltdown
> The melting of a nuclear reactor core.

nuclear fission
> The act of splitting the nucleus of an atom to produce a nuclear reaction and release energy for power.

nuclear reactor
> A machine in a nuclear power plant that produces power.

radioactive
> Giving off harmful radiation, which can cause health problems such as birth defects and cancer.

refinery
> A factory that turns crude oil into gasoline or other usable products.

renewable energy
> Energy that is produced from sources that cannot be depleted, or used up, such as the sun or the wind.

reserve
> The amount of oil that can be produced within a given period of time.

sanction
> Action, such as economic or trade, taken by one or more nations to force another nation to act a certain way. These include denying foreign aid and restricting imports and exports.

SOURCE NOTES

Chapter 1. The Rising Cost of Oil
1. H. Josef Hebert. "$2 gas: Get used to it: Government predicts high prices through next year." *Decatur Daily News* 8 Apr. 2005. 25 Mar. 2008 <http://legacy.decaturdaily.com/decaturdaily/news/050408/gas.shtml>.
2. Justin Blum. "An Easily Threatened Oil Industry: A Storm or Terrorist Attack Anywhere Could Disrupt Supplies Globally," *Washington Post* 21 Sept. 2005: D01. 25 Mar. 2008 <http://www.washingtonpost.com/wp-dyn/content/article/2005/09/20/AR2005092001791.html>.

Chapter 2. Signs Pointing to an Oil Crisis
1. John Cassidy. "Pump Dreams." *The New Yorker* 11 Oct. 2004. 16 Mar. 2008 <http://www.newyorker.com/archive/2004/10/11/041011fa_fact?currentPage=all>.
2. Brian Carr. "Have Sustained High Gas Prices Changed Your Driving?" *Daily Fuel Economy Tip.* 17 Oct. 2007. 16 Mar. 2008 <http://www.dailyfueleconomytip.com/drive-less/have-sustained-high-gas-prices-changed-your-driving/>.
3. L. F. Ivanhoe. "Get Ready for Another Oil Shock" *Futurist* Jan/Feb97, 31:1. 20–23. 16 Mar. 2008 <http://dieoff.org/page90.htm>.
4. L. F. Ivanhoe. "Future World Oil Supplies: There Is a Finite Limit," *World Oil* Oct. 95: 77–88. 16 Mar. 2008 <http://dieoff.org/page85.htm>.
5. Matthew Simmons. Transcript of Interview with Lise Doucette. "Saudi Oil Shortage," *Global Public Media.* 3 Aug. 2005. 16 Mar. 2008 <http://globalpublicmedia.com/transcripts/459>.
6. John Attarian. "Oil Depletion Revisited: Why the Peak Is Probably Near." *The Social Contract* Winter 2004–2005: 129–146. 25 Mar. 2008 <http://www.thesocialcontract.com/artman2/publish/tsc1502/article_1290.shtml>.
7. Ibid.
8. David R. Francis. "Has global oil production peaked?" *Christian Science Monitor.* 29 Jan. 2004. 16 Mar. 2008 <http://www.csmonitor.com/2004/0129/p14s01-wogi.html>.

Chapter 3. Signs Pointing to No Oil Crisis

1. Peter W. Huber and Mark P. Mills. *The Bottomless Well*. New York: Basic Books, 2005. xv.
2. Walter E. Williams. "Running Out of Oil?" *HumanEvents.com*. 19 July 2006. 25 Mar. 2007 <http://www.humanevents.com/article.php?id=16084&keywords=oil%2C+reserves>.
3. Jimmy Carter. "The President's Proposed Energy Policy." 18 Apr. 1977. Vital Speeches of the Day, 43:14 (1977): 418–420. 2002. *American Experience*, PBS Online/WGBH. 25 Mar. 2008 <http://www.pbs.org/wgbh/amex/carter/filmmore/ps_energy.html>.
4. Leonardo Maugeri. "Two Cheers for Expensive Oil." *Foreign Affairs*. Mar.-Apr. 2006: 150.
5. Ibid. 152.
6. Jad Mouawad. "Oil Innovations Pump New Life Into Old Wells," *New York Times* 5 Mar. 2007. 25 Mar. 2008 <http://www.nytimes.com/2007/03/05/business/05oil1.html>.

Chapter 4. Politics of Oil: U.S. Domestic Policies

1. George W. Bush. "President's Statement on the Energy Policy Act of 2005." The White House. 8 Aug. 2005. 25 Mar. 2008 <http://www.whitehouse.gov/news/releases/2005/08/20050808-9.html>.
2. Caspar W. Weinberger. "An Energy Bill—At Last." *Forbes*. 3 Oct. 2005. 25 Mar. 2008 <http://members.forbes.com/forbes/2005/1003/035.html>.
3. Jimmy Carter. "The President's Proposed Energy Policy." 18 Apr. 1977. *Vital Speeches of the Day*, 43:14 (1977): 418–420. 2002. *American Experience*, PBS Online/WGBH. 25 Mar. 2008 <http://www.pbs.org/wgbh/amex/carter/filmmore/ps_energy.html>.
4. Justin Blum. "Bill Wouldn't Wean U.S. Off Oil Imports, Analysts Say," *Washington Post* 26 July 2005: A01.
5. Ibid.
6. Ron Gettelfinger. "Improving Fuel Economy." *New York Times* 6 Oct. 2007. 25 Mar. 2008 <http://query.nytimes.com/gst/fullpage.html?res=9E0DE2DD173EF935A35753C1A9619C8B63>.

Source Notes Continued

Chapter 5. Politics of Oil: International Relations
1. Michael T. Klare. *Blood and Oil*. New York: Metropolitan Books. 2004. xvi.
2. Anthony H. Cordesman and Khalid R. Al-Rodhan. *The Global Oil Market: Risks and Uncertainties*. Washington, DC: The CSIS Press. 2006. 76.
3. Thomas L. Friedman. "Too Much Pork and Too Little Sugar," *New York Times* 5 Aug. 2005. 25 Mar. 2008
<http://www.nytimes.com/2005/08/05/opinion/
05friedman.html?_r=1&oref=slogin>.
4. Andrea C. Nakaya. *Oil*. Detroit: Thomson Gale, 2006. 191.
5. Ibid. 162.

Chapter 6. Oil and the Environment
1. Andrew C. Revkin. "National Briefing: Science and Health: Carbon Dioxide Emissions Down," *New York Times* 24 May 2007. 25 Mar. 2008 <http://query.nytimes.com/gst/fullpage.html?res=
9B00EEDC1630F937A15756C0A9619C8B63>.
2. Ross Gelbspan. "Michael Crichton's Misstated State of Fear." *National Wildlife*. Apr.–May 2005: 12.
3. Al Gore. *An Inconvenient Truth*. Emmaus, PA: Rodale, 2006. 214.
4. "Nobel Peace Prize 2007" *Nobel Foundation*. 2007. 25 Mar. 2008.
<http://nobelprize.org/nobel_prizes/peace/laureates/2007/>.
5. Al Gore. *An Inconvenient Truth*. Emmaus, PA: Rodale, 2006. 196.

Chapter 7. Carbon-free Energy
1. Patrick Moore. "Going Nuclear: A Green Makes the Case," *Washington Post* 16 Apr. 2006. B01.

Chapter 8. Arguments Supporting Alternative Energy Use
1. Tom Solon, "It Is All About Power: Nuclear Energy Should Be Our Main Power Source." *Design News* 21 Feb. 2005: 16. 25 Mar. 2008 <http://www.designnews.com/article/CA503761.html?indus
tryid=22203&text=It%27s+all+about+power>.

Chapter 9. Arguments Against Alternative Energy Use
1. "Consider the Alternatives." *Economist* 30 Apr. 2005: 21.
2. Ibid.
3. Steven Ashley. "On the road to fuel-cell cars." *Scientific American* Mar. 2005: 62.

Chapter 10. Solutions That Bridge the Gap
1. Michael D. Lemonick. "How to kick the oil habit." *Time* 31 Oct. 2005: 60.
2. "M. King Hubbert." *HubbertPeak.com*. 2007. 25 Feb. 2008 <http://www.hubbertpeak.com/hubbert/>.
3. "USGS: 25% Arctic oil, gas estimate a reporter's mistake." *Petroleum News* 21 Oct. 2007. 25 Mar. 2008 <http://www.petroleumnews.com/pntruncate/347702651.shtml>.
4. "Fate of ANWR Hangs in the Balance." *Greenpeace.org*. 16 Mar. 2006. 25 Mar. 2008 <http://www.greenpeace.org/usa/news/anwr>.
5. Mac Johnson. "Prudhoe Bay Shutdown Involves Less Than Half of Likely ANWR Reserves." *Human Events* 14 Aug. 2006: 9.
6. Charles Krauthammer. "Energy Independence?" *Washington Post* 26 Jan. 2007: A21.
7. Michael D. Lemonick. "How to kick the oil habit." *Time* 31 Oct. 2005: 60.
8. Norma Carr-Ruffino and John Acheson. "The Hybrid Phenomenon." *Futurist* July-Aug. 2007: 17.
9. Ibid. 22.
10. "Ethanol is Not the Answer: Stop Global Warming." *Greenpeace.org*. 8 Mar. 2007. 25 Mar. 2008 <http://www.greenpeace.org/usa/news/ethanol-is-not-the-answer-sto>.

INDEX

About the Author

Jill Sherman is the editor of several nonfiction children's books. She has a bachelor's degree in English from the College of New Jersey. Jill resides in Minneapolis, Minnesota. This is her first book.

Photo Credits

Charlie Riedel/AP Images, cover, 67, 95; Ed Andrieski/AP Images, 6; Red Line Editorial, 10, 13; Peter Cosgrove/AP Images, 15; Greg Baker/AP Images, 16; Tao Ming/AP Images, 19; Zavoral Libor/ AP Images, 25; Mike Kepka/San Francisco Chronicle/Corbis, 26; Kamran Jebreili/AP Images, 30; Marcio Jose Sanchez/AP Images, 33; Gene J. Puskar/AP Images, 34; J. Scott Applewhite/AP Images, 37; Paul Sancya/AP Images, 41; Reuters/Corbis, 42; Hasan Jamali/AP Images, 47; Buck Lau/epa/Corbis, 51; Jack Smith/AP Images, 52; Rob Stapleton/AP Images, 55; Manu Fernandez/AP Images, 59; Frank Rumpenhorst/AP Images, 60; Jackie Johnston/ AP Images, 65; George Steinmetz/Corbis, 68; Wang huaiqiu/ Imaginechina/AP Images, 73; David Vincent/AP Images, 74; Lennox McLendon/AP Images, 81; AP Images, 82; Toyota/AP Images, 89; David Sailors/Corbis, 93